Peaceful Journey

Piano compositions from the Peaceful Journey Series

by
Cynthia Jordan

copyright 1999 by Emerald Eagle Music
All songs registered with ASCAP
International Copyright Secured All Rights Reserved

*Music is the universal language
that speaks to our hearts
and expresses the quiet secrets of our souls.*

Thank you for allowing me to share my music with you.

Love, Cynthia

*This book is fondly dedicated to my beloved Grandmother, Tita.
Tita bought me my first piano and taught me the beauty of unconditional love.*

Musical Index

Music is the organized flow of harmonic energy, which profoundly resonates with the human spirit. When I compose music, I think of it as audio poetry, spiritually communicating to the soul, the passionate expression of life in motion.
~ Cynthia

A Mother's Heart   page 6
This melody is an expression of my intimate understanding of motherhood.
I wrote it in the spirit of my grandmother, Tita.

Autumn Equinox   page 8
An old Indian legend tells a tale of how at one time all the trees were green. Some were jealous of the beautiful colors of the flowers and asked Great Spirit to change their foliage to brilliant colors. Their wish was granted, but because of their vanity they would pay the price of becoming barren and ugly during the cold winter. The evergreens happily stayed content as God created them. I wrote this piece one morning in October, while watching brilliant, colored leaves fall to the ground.

Encantada   page 14
Encantada is the Spanish word for enchanted. The beauty of the ocean inspired this composition. When I gaze upon her horizon I have a feeling of great adventure and endless possibilities. Like a beautiful woman, her cycles are determined by sister moon and her depth holds mysterious secrets known only to her heart.

Fiona's Dream   page 18
Fiona's Dream, was inspired by a fictional character in Morgan Llewelyn's, Lion of Ireland, the story of Brian Boru. In the book Fiona was a woman from the old religion who held magical powers. She loved Brian and seemed to know when he needed her special magic and wisdom. It is dedicated to the quiet strength of all women.

Quiet Journey   page 24
This melody is an invitation for you to go on a peaceful journey within your mind. Remember that everyday has the potential of unlimited possibilities!

First Light of Dawn   page 28   poem page 27
Every day brings a fresh, new beginning and there is always the unlimited potential for anything to happen. The brilliant colors of the dawn are like fire in the sky and the beauty seems to hold a soft powerful energy. I get a secure feeling that says, "life goes on" as I watch the darkness fade away and the brilliant sun shine through, to light the new day.

Great Glen   page 34
As I wrote this piece, I imagined myself on the Highlands of Scotland. I saw a young beautiful lass singing as she gathered wild flowers on the hillside. A young man sitting on a white steed was watching her from his view on the hill. His heart was full as he looked upon the fair maiden. The magic of imagination can take you to any time or place.

Kincora   page 43
The story of Brian Boru has touched me deeply at a soulful level. Kincora is the name given to Brian's magnificent castle in Ireland. As I created this piece, I imagined myself in the 11th century, as a lady in the king's court, celebrating with dining and dancing within the stonewalls of Kincora, as the Shannon River flowed nearby, singing her song.

Sagesse   page 48
Sagesse is the French word for "wisdom". Old things are beautiful because they seem to possess a quiet knowing. I love places like Rome, because as I look upon the remains left from another time, I wonder what stories these things would tell if they could speak. We are all students of life and I see "old" people as amazing, because they have "sagesse".

Sedona   page 52
Native Americans think of Sedona, Arizona as a place of magical power. Its beautiful desert landscape is decorated with deep reds and rich earth colors, giving it a spiritual ambience. Some even believe that Sedona was a Mecca at the time of Atlantis. Many people visit Sedona in the search of spiritual enlightenment and healing. It is one the most beautiful places I have ever seen on earth.

Serena   page 56
Serena is the Latin word for serenity. Is there a place you know that when you are there you feel a soft sense of peace and tranquility? Maybe it's a memory from your childhood. I invite you to go there in your mind as you play this melody.

The Emerald Valley   page 60
When I think of the Misty Isles I cannot help but envision a deep color of emerald green. I am in awe of nature when I witness the view of a beautiful green valley from the mountains above. Green is the color of the earth's abundance and all the gifts she gives.

The Shannon   page 64
The Shannon is the main river that flows through Ireland. The ancient Celts threw their treasures in rivers as a gift of thanksgiving for nurturing their crops. They had a strong reverence to water as they saw it as a source of nourishment and life. An old Irish lullaby is woven into the arrangement because I think of rivers as singing a song of peace.

Vernal Equinox   page 70
The Vernal equinox is the day that marks the end of winter and the beginning of spring. It is one of the two days of the year that night and day are equal in length and occurs around March 21st. It is an exciting and beautiful time of year as the dormant awakes into pastels and deep greens and the creative cycle of life renews itself once again.

Santiago   page 74
This composition is a tribute to the "Santiago," also known as the El Camino, a road known as a spiritual pilgrimage in the countryside of Spain. For hundreds of years, people from all over the world walk the Santiago to closer connect with God.

Autumn Equinox

Cynthia Jordan

Encantada

Cynthia Jordan

With open space

copyright 1999 by Emerald Eagle Music ASCAP www.cynthiamusic.com
International Copyright Secured All Rights Reserved

Enchantment fills my soul
When I experience
The beautiful feeling of oneness
With all of God's creations

Fiona's Dream

Cynthia Jordan

copyright 1999 by Emerald Eagle Music ASCAP www.cynthiamusic.com
International Copyright Secured All Rights Reserved

Magical scenes with timeless adventures
Exist in the hours of slumber
Ah, beautiful Fiona
Bring your magic to light
As you allow dreams to manifest
In the field of existence
Mortals know as the day

Cynthia

Quiet Journey

Cynthia Jordan

The First Light of Dawn

It is the darkest hour.
You can hear the silent voice of the night
as the land waits patiently for her arrival.
She will come… She always does.
Quietly at first, the sweet songs
of small-feathered minstrels fill the air
as if announcing, "Her Majesty is approaching!"
From the east a soft glow of light
can be seen on the horizon.
Then, subtly, before all
who have the privilege to witness,
the sky is transformed into an exquisite masterpiece!
The lady, being quite the lady,
very slowly reveals her beauty with grace and style.
Bright magentas and brilliant colors
of fiery orange and gold, exhibit her passions
as she paints a magnificent picture of endless beauty!!
My breath is taken away… She is here!
Her heavenly essence seeks no approval
as she generously lights the new day,
a new beginning for all.
She is not selective and gives unconditionally
as she embraces all of life with her warmth and light.
Her lovely golden rays shimmer through the forest trees
and shine boldly through the clouds.
A gentle peace fills my soul
at the First Light of Dawn.

Cynthia Jordan

First Light of Dawn

Cynthia Jordan

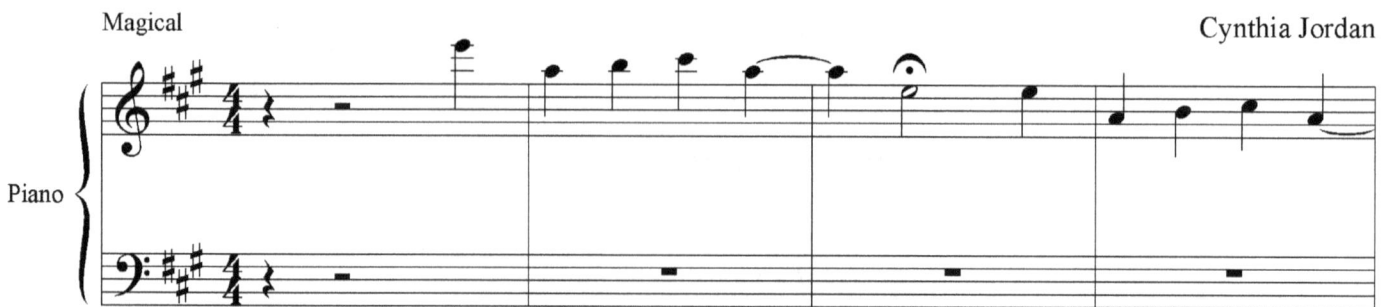

copyright 1999 by Emerald Eagle Music ASCAP www.cynthiamusic.com
International Copyright Secured All Rights Reserved

The Great Glen

Cynthia Jordan

copyright 1999 by Emerald Eagle Music ASCAP www.cynthiamusic.com
International Copyright Secured All Rights Reserved

Sagesse

Cynthia Jordan

copyright 1999 by Emerald Eagle Music ASCAP www.cynthiamusic.com
International Copyright Secured All Rights Reserved

Sedona

Mystic Knowing

Cynhia Jordan

53

Serena

Cynthia Jordan

copyright 1999 by Emerald Eagle Music ASCAP www.cynthiamusic.com
International Copyright Secured All Rights Reserved

Peace, love and joy
Fill my soul
When my silent thoughts disappear
And I listen only
To the language of my heart
Ah, Serena

The Emerald Valley

Cynthia Jordan

copyright 1999 by Emerald Eagle Music ASCAP www.cynthiamusic.com
International Copyright Secured All Rights Reserved

May there always be work for your hands to do;
May your purse always hold a coin or two;
May the sun always shine on your windowpane;
May a rainbow be certain to follow each rain;
May the hand of a friend always be near you;
May God fill your heart with gladness to cheer you.

The Shannon

Cynthia Jordan

Flowing

*The Shenandoah River in Virginia was named by the early American Irish settlers
in honor of the Shannon River in Ireland.
The beautiful, green terrain reminded them of their homeland that they dearly loved.*

Vernal Equinox

Cynthia Jordan

copyright 1999 by Emerald Eagle Music ASCAP www.cynthiamusic.com
International Copyright Secured All Rights Reserved

Santiago

Cynthia Jordan

With passion

Piano

www.ingramcontent.com/pod-product-compliance
Lightning Source LLC
Chambersburg PA
CBHW050750100426
42744CB00012BA/1955